W9-BVU-554

Please remember that this is a library book,
and that it belongs only temporarily to each
person who uses it. Be considerate. Do
not write in this, or any, library book.

Great Americana

A Brief History of the Pequot War

John Mason

.

A Brief History
of the Pequot War

by John Mason

READEX MICROPRINT

Foreword

In order to bring to an end both the Pequots' continual harassment of the new settlers and their plans for a great Indian confederation which might include the large Narragansett tribe, the Connecticut authorities in May of 1637 took the offensive against the Pequots. The man placed in command of the troops was John Mason, a recent settler who had gained his experience fighting with Fairfax in the Netherlands. The ensuing war resulted in the annihilation of the Pequots. It became clear to other potentially hostile Indians, who had always feared the Pequots more than they did the English, that the colonists were ready to fight when necessary.

As early as 1638 two separate histories of the war, one by John Underhill and the other by Philip Vincent, appeared in print. In 1656, nineteen years after the events, the General Court of Connecticut requested John Mason to write his own eye witness account since, "History most properly is a declaration of things that are done by those that were present at the doing of them." Because there were discrepancies as to the conduct of the war in the earlier versions written soon after the heat of battle, Mason viewed his task as "...not so much to stir up the affections of men, as to declare in truth and plainness the actions and doings of men: I shall therefore set down matters in order as they began and were carried on and issued."

Increase Mather in 1677 printed *A Relation of the Troubles That Have Hapned in New England* and included in it a portion of Mason's manuscript. Mather, however, believed it to be the work of John Allyn and so it was not until the Boston, 1736 edition, reprinted here, that Mason was identified as the author. *A Brief History of the Pequot War... In 1637: Written by Major John Mason, A principal Actor therein, as then chief Captain and Commander of Connecticut Forces*, one of the four classical contemporary histories of the war, includes an introductory sketch of Mason's life by Thomas Prince, relates the actions which prompted open conflict, and describes the movements of the troops leading up to and including the surprise attack at "Mistick" where more than 700 Pequots were slain. Charles Orr edited and reprinted the four tracts by Mason, Underhill, Vincent, and Lion Gardiner in a single volume called *History of the Pequot War* (Cleveland, 1897). Louis Bond Mason has written *The Life and Times of Major John Mason of Connecticut* (New York, 1935).

A Brief History of the Pequot War

A
Brief Hiftory
OF THE
𝕻equot 𝖂ar:
Efpecially
Of the memorable *Taking* of their FORT at
MISTICK in CONNECTICUT
In
1 6 3 7.

Written by

Major *John Mason*,

A principal Actor therein, as then chief *Captain* and *Commander* of *Connecticut Forces.*

With an *Introduction* and fome Explanatory *Notes*
By the Reverend
Mr. THOMAS PRINCE.

Pfal. xliv. 1--3 *We have heard with our Ears, O* GOD, *our Fathers have told us, what Work Thou didft in their Days, in the times of old. How Thou dift drive out the Heathen with thy Hand, and plantedft Them: how Thou did afflict the People and caft them out. For they got not the Land in Poffeffion by their own Sword, neither did their own Arm fave them: but thy right Hand, and thine Arm, and the Light of thy Countenance, becaufe Thou hadft a Favour unto them.*
Pfal. cii. 18. *This fhall be written for the Generation to come; and the People which fhall be Created, fhall Praife the* LORD.

BOSTON: Printed & Sold by. S. KNEELAND & T. GREEN in Queen-ftreet, 1736.

INTRODUCTION.

I N my Contemplations of the DIVINE PROVIDENCE towards the People of *New-England*, I have often tho't what a special Favour it was, that there came over with the first Settlers of *Plimouth* & *Connecticut Colonies*, which in those Times were especially exposed to the superiour Power of the *Barbarians* round about them ; *Two brave Englishmen* bred to Arms in the *Dutch Netherlands*, viz. Capt. MILES STANDISH of *Plimouth*, and Capt JOHN MASON of *Connecticut*: Gentlemen of tried Valour, Military Skill and Conduct, great Activity, and warm Zeal for that noble Cause of *Pure Scriptural Religion*, and *Religious Liberty*, which were the chief original Design and Interest of *the Fathers of those Plantations* ; and who were acted with such eminent Degrees of Faith and Piety, as excited them to the most daring Enterprizes in the Cause of GOD and of *his People*, and went a great way to their wonderful Successes.

Like those inspired *Heroes* of whom we read the History in the *Eleventh* Chapter to the HEBREWS--*By Faith*, they not only *rather chose to suffer Affliction with the People of* GOD *than to enjoy the Pleasures of Sin for a Season* ; *esteeming the Reproach of* CHRIST *greater Riches than the Treasures of Egypt* : But *by Faith they even forsook the same, passed thro' the Sea, subdued Kingdoms, wrought Righteousness, obtained Promises, waxed valiant in Fight, and turned to Flight the Armies of the Aliens.*

The Judicious Reader that knows the *New Englijh* Hiftory, cannot think thefe *Scripture Phrafes* or religious Turns unfuitable on this
Occafion: For as *thefe Colonies* were chiefly, if not entirely Settled
by a *Religious People,* and for *thofe Religious Purpofes*; It is as impoffible to write an impartial or true Hiftory of *them,* as of the ancient
Ifraelites, or the later *Vaudois* or *North-Britons,* without obferving
that *Religious Spirit and Intention* which evidently run thro' and
animate their Hiftorical Tranfactions.

Capt. STANDISH was of a lower Stature, but of fuch a daring
and active Genius, that even before the Arrival of the *Maffachufetts
Colony,* He fpread a Terror over all the Tribes of *Indians* round about
him, from the *Maffachufetts* to *Martha's Vineyard,* & from *Cape-Cod Harbour* to *Narraganfett.* Capt. MASON was Tall and Portly, but never
the lefs full of Martial Bravery and Vigour; thatHe foon became
the equal Dread of the more numerous Nations from *Narraganfett*
to *Hudfon's River.* They were BOTH the Inftrumental Saviours of
this Country in the moft critical Conjunctures: And as we quietly
enjoy the Fruits of their extraordinary Diligence and Valour, both
the prefent and future Generations will for ever be obliged to revere
their Memory.

Capt. MASON, the Writer of the following Hiftory, in which He
was a principal Actor, as Chief Commander of the *Connecticut* Forces,
is faid to have been a Relative of Mr. *John Mafon* the ancient *Clai-
mer* of the *Province of New-Hampfhire*: However, the *Captain* was
one of the firft who went up from the *Maffachufetts* about the Year
1635 to lay the Foundation of CONNECTICUT COLONY: He went
from *Dorchefter,* firft fettled at *Windfor,* and thence marched forth to
the *Pequot War.*

But it being above *Threefcore Years* fince the following Narrative
was Written, near *an Hundred* fince the Events therein related, and
the State of the *New England Colonies* being long fince greatly Chang-
ed; it feems needful for the prefent Readers clearer Apprehenfion
of thefe Matters, to Obferve--That in the Year 1633, & 1634, feveral
Englifhmen arriving from *England,* at the *Maffachufetts,* went up in
the Weftern Country to difcover *Connecticut River*; the *next Year*
began to remove thither; and by the Beginning of 1637, *Hartford,
Windfor* and *Weathersfield* were Settled, befides a *Fortification* built
at *Saybrook* on the Mouth of the River.

At that Time there were efpecially *three* powerful and warlike
Nations of *Indians* in the *SouthWeftern* Parts of *New-England*; which
fpread

fpread all the Country from *Aquethneck*, fince call'd *Rhode-Ifland*, to *Quinnepiack*, fince called *New-Haven* ; viz. the NARRAGANSETTS, PEQUOTS and MOHEGANS. The NARRAGANSETTS reached from the Bay of the fame Name, to *Pawcatuck River*, now the Boundary between the Governments of *Rhode-Ifland* and *Connecticut* : And their Head Sachem was MIANTONIMO. The PEQUOTS reached from thence Weftward to *Connecticut River*, and over it, as far as *Branford*, if not *Quinnepiack* ; their Head Sachem being SASSACUS. And the MOHEGANS fpread along from the *Narraganfetts* thro' the Inland Country, on the Back or Northerly Side of the *Pequots*, between *them* and the *Nipmucks* ; their Head Sachem being UNCAS.

The moft terrible of all thofe Nations were then the PEQUOTS ; who with their *depending Tribes* foon entered on a Refolution to Deftroy the *Englifh* out of the Country. In 1634, they killed Capt. *Stone* and all his Company, being *feven* befides Himfelf, in & near his Bark on *Connecticut River*. In 1635, they killed Capt. *Oldham* in his Bark at *Block-Ifland* ; and at *Long-Ifland* they killed *two* more caft away there. In 1636, and the following *Winter* and *March*, they killed *fix* & took *feven* more at *Connecticut River* : Thofe they took alive they tortured to Death in a moft barbarous Manner. And on *April* 23. 1637, they killed *nine* more and carried *two* young Women Captive at *Weatherfield*.

They had earneftly folicited the *Narraganfetts* to engage in their Confederacy : very politickly reprefenting to them, *That if they fhou'd help or fuffer the* Englifh *to fubdue the* Pequots, *they wou'd thereby make Way for their own future Ruin ; and that they need not come to open Battle with the* Englifh *; only Fire our Houfes, kill our Cattle, lye in Ambufh and fhoot us as we went about our Bufinefs ; fo we fhould be quickly forced to leave this Country, and the* Indians *not expofed to any great Hazard.* Thofe truly politick Arguments were upon the Point of prevailing on the *Narraganfetts* : And had *Thefe* with the *Mohegans*, to whom the *Pequots* were nearly related, join'd againft us ; they might *then*, in the infant State of thefe Colonies, have eafily accomplifhed their defparate Refolutions.

But the *Narraganfetts* being more afraid of the *Pequots* than of the *Englifh* ; were willing they fhou'd weaken each other, not in the leaft imagining the *Englifh* cou'd deftroy *them* ; at the fame time an *Agency* from the *Maffachufetts Colony* to the *Narraganfetts*, happily Preferved their ftaggering Friendfhip. And as UNCAS the Great Sachim of the *Moheags*, upon the firft coming of the *Englifh*, fell into

into an intimate Acquaintance with Capt. *Mason*, He from the Beginning entertained us in an amicable Manner : And tho' both by *his Father and Mother* He derived from the *Royal Blood* of the *Pequots*, and had Married the *Daughter* of TATOBAM their then late Sachim; yet fuch was his Affection for us, as he faithfully adhered to us, ventured his Life in our Service, affifted at the Taking their *Fort*, when about *Seven Hundred* of them were Deftroyed, and thereupon in fubduing and driving out of the Country the remaining greater Part of that fierce and dangerous Nation.

Soon after the War, Capt. *Mason* was by the Government of *Connecticut*, made the *Major General* of all their Forces, and fo continued to the Day of his Death : The Rev. Mr. HOOKER of *Hartford*, being defired by the Government in their Name to deliver *the Staff* into his Hand ; We may imagin he did it with that fuperiourPiety, Spirit and Majefty, which were peculiar to him : Like an ancient Prophet addreffing himfelf to the Military Officer, delivering to him the Principal Enfign of Martial Power, to Lead the Armies & Fight the Battles of the LORD and of *his People*.

Major *Mason* having been trained up in the *Netherland War* under Sir THOMAS FAIRFAX; when the Struggle arofe in *England* between K. *Charles* I. and the *Parliament* about the Royal Powers and the National Liberties; *that Famous General* had fuch an Efteem for the *Major's* Conduct and Bravery, that *He* wrote to the *Major* to come over and help *Him*. But the *Major* excufing himfelf, continued in this Country as long as he lived, and had fome of the greateft Honours his *Colony* cou'd yield him.

For befides his Office of *Major General*, the Colony in *May* 1660 chofe him their DEPUTY GOVERNOUR; continued him in the fame Poft by annual Re-elections, by virtue of their firft Conftitution to 1662 inclufively. The *fame Year* K. CHARLES II. comprehending the *Colonies* of *Connecticut* and *NewHaven* in *One Government* by the Name of CONNECTICUT COLONY ; He in the *Royal Charter*, figned *April* 23, appointed Major *Mason* their firft *Deputy Governour* till the *fecond Thurfday* of *October* following : After which, the *General Court* being left to chufe their Officers, they continued to chufe him their *Deputy Governour* every Year to *May* 1670 ; when his Age and Bodily Infirmities advancing, he laid down his Office and retired from Publick Bufinefs.

After the *Pequot War*, he had removed from *Windfor* to *Saybrook* : But in 1659, he removed thence to *Norwich* ; where he *Died* in 1672, or or 16͞73,in the 73d Year of hisAge : leaving *three Sons*, viz. *Samuel*, *John* and *Daniel*, to imitate their Father's Example and inherit his Virtues.

I have only now to obferve, that in *The Relation of the Troubles which happened to* New England *by the* Indians *from* 1614 *to* 1675, Publifhed by the then Mr. INCREASE MATHER in 1677, I find a *Copy* of the *following Narrative*, but without the Prefaces, had been communicated to him by Mr. *John Allyn* then the *Secretary* of *Connecticut Colony* ; which that Rev. Author took for Mr. *Allyn's*, and calls it *his.* But we muft inform the Reader, that *the Narrative* was originally drawn by Major *Mafon.* And as *his Eldeft Grandfon* Capt. *John Mafon* now of *New-London* has put it into my Hands ; I have been more than ufually careful in Correcting the Prefs according to the *Original* ; as *the moft authentick Account* of the *Pequot War*, and as a *ftanding Monument* both of the extraordinary Dangers & Courage of our pious *Fathers* & of the eminentAppearance of HEAVEN to fave them.

' The *other Actions* of Major *Mafon* muft be referred to the *Genera͞l*
' *Hiftory* of *this Country*, when fome Gentleman of greater Qualifica-
' tions and Leifure than I may claim, fhall rife up among us, to
' undertake it.   I fhall give fome Hints in my *Brief Chronology* ;
' which thro' numerous Hindrances, is now in fuch a Forwardnefs,
' that near 200 *Pages* are Printed already ; and in a little Time,
' Life and Health allow'd, I hope to prefent the Publick with the
' *firft* of the *two* intended *Volumns.* In the mean while I cannot but
' Regret it, that fuch confiderable and ancient Towns as *Saybrook*,
' *Fairfield*, *Stamford*, *Canterbury*, *Groton* in the County of *Middlefex*,
' *Chelmsford*, *Billerica*, *Wcburn*, *Dunftable* and *Briftol*,fhould afford no
' more than their *bare Names* in the Publifhed Records of this
' Country.

Bofton, Dec. 23.
    1735.   *Thomas Prince.*

∾◌◌∾◌◌∾◌◌∾◌∾◌◌♣◌∾◌◌♣◌∾◌◌♣◌∾◌◌♣◌∾◌◌∾◌◌∾

N. B. The only Word left out is *my* in Dedication, Page i͞ᴣ where it fhould be Read---*My own Unfitnefs* : the *few Mifpel-lings* are only of the *Englifh Words* ; which with the *Mifpoint-ings*, are eafily Deferned and Corrected.

TO

The Honourable

The General Court
of *Connecticut*.

Honoured Gentlemen,

OU well know how often I have been re-quefted by your felves to write fomething in reference to the Subject of the enfuing Treatife (who have power to Command) and how backward I have been, as being confcious to own unfitnefs ; accounting it not fo proper, I being a Chief Actor therein my felf. Yet confidering that little hath been done to keep the Memory of fuch a fpecial Providence alive, though I could heartily have wifhed that fome other who had been lefs interefted and better qualified might have undertaken the Task, for I am not unacquainted with my own Weaknefs ; yet I fhall endeavour in plainnefs and faithfulnefs impartially to declare the Matter, not taking the Crown from the Head of one and putting it upon another. There are feveral who have Wrote and alfo Printed at random

B

on this Subject, greatly miffing the Mark in many Things
as I conceive. I shall not exempt my self from frail-
ties, yet from material Faults I presume you may pro-
nounce it not Guilty, and do assure you that if I should
see or by any be convinced of an Error, I shall at once
confess and amend it.

I thought it my Duty in the Entrance to relate the
firft Grounds *upon which the* Englifh *took up Arms*
againft the Pequots ; *for the* Beginning is the Moiety
of the Whole ; *and not to mention some Paffages at*
Rovers, *as others have done, and not demonftrate the*
Caufe. *Judge of me as you pleafe : I shall not climb*
after Applaufe, nor do I much fear a Cenfure ; there
being many Teftimonies *to what I shall say.* 'Tis
poffible some may think no better can be expected in
thefe diftracting Times ; it being so hard to pleafe a
few, impoffible to pleafe all : I shall therefore content
my self that I have attended my Rule : You may
pleafe to improve some others who were Actors in the
Service to give in their Apprehenfions, that so the se-
verals being compared, you may inlarge or diminifh as
you shall see meet. I defire my Name may be sparingly
mentioned : My principal Aim is that God *may have*
his due Praife.

By your unworthy Servant,

John Mafon.

TO THE

American Reader.

Judicious Reader,

*A*LTHOUGH *it be too true indeed that the Press labours under, and the World doth too much abound with pamphleting Papers; yet know that this Piece cannot or at least ought not to be disaccepted by thee: For by the help of this thou mayest look backward and interpret how* GOD *hath been working, and that very wonderfully for thy Safety and Comfort: And it being the* LORD'S *doing, it should be* marvellous in thine Eyes.

And when thou shalt have viewed over this Paper, thou wilt say the Printers of this Edition have done well to prevent the possible Imputation of Posterity; in that they have consulted the exhibition at least to the American World, of the remarkable Providences of GOD, *which thou mayest at thy leisure read, consider and affect thy self with, in the Sequel.*

History *most properly is a Declaration of Things that are done by those that were present at the doing of*

B 2 *them:*

them : *Therefore this here presented to thee may in that respect plead for liking and acceptance with thee :* *The* Historiographer *being one of the principal Actors, by whom those* English *Engagements were under* GOD *carried on and so successfully effected.* *And for a* President *for him in th's his Publication of his own,* in Parte Rei Bellicæ, *he hath that great Man at Arms the* first *of the noble* Cæsars, *being the Manager and Inditer of his martial Exploits.*

He has *also that necessary Ingredient in an* Historian ; Ut nequid falsi dicere, et nequid veri non dicere audeat ; *That he will tell the Truth and will not say a jot of Falshood.*

And Memorandum *that those divine Over-rulings, their Recollection, as they ought to be Quickeners of us up to a Theological Reformation, and Awakeners of us from a lethargilike Security, least the Lord should yet again make them more afflicting* Thorns in our Eyes *and flashing Scourges in our Sides ; so also they may well be* Pledges *or Earnests to us of his future saving Mercies ; and that if we by our Declensions from him in his ways do not provoke him, he will not forsake us, but have respect to us in our Dwellings, and lend us the desirable Providence of his perpetual Salvation.*

N. B. This Epistle to the AMERICAN READER appears to have been written by another Hand than *Major Mason's*

TO

(v)

TO THE

Judicious Reader.

Gentlemen,

Never had thought that this should have come to the Press, until of late : If I had, I should have endeavoured to have put a little more Varnish upon it : But being over perswaded by some Friends, I thought it not altogether amiss to present it to your courteous Disposition, hoping it might find your favourable Entertainment and Acceptance, though rude and impolish'd. I wish it had fallen into some better Hands that might have performed it to the Life : I shall only draw the Curtain and open my little Casement, that so others of larger Hearts and Abilities may let in a biger Light ; that so at least some small Glimmering may be left to Posterity what Difficulties and Obstructions their Forefathers met with in their first settling these desart Parts of America; how GOD was pleased to prove them, and how by his wise Providence he ordered and disposed all their Occasions and Affairs for them in regard to both their Civils and Ecclesiasticals.

This with some other Reasons have been Motives to excite me to the enterprizing hereof; no Man that I know of having as yet undertaken to write a general History or
'Relation ;

Relation; so that there is no Commemoration *of Matters respecting* this War; *how they began, how carried on, and continued nor what Success they had.* * *They which think the mentioning of some Particulars is sufficient for the understanding of the General, in my Opinion stray no less from the Truth, then if by the separated Parts of a living Man one should think by this Means he knew all the Parts and Perfections of the Creature: But these separated Parts being joyned together having Form and Life, one might easily discern that he was deceived.*

If the Beginning be but obscure and the Ground uncertain, its Continuance can hardly perswade to purchase Belief : Or if Truth be wanting in History, *it proves but a fruitless Discourse.*

I shall therefore, God *helping, endeavour not so much to stir up the Affections of* Men, *as to declare in Truth and Plainness the Actions and Doings of* Men: *I shall therefore set down Matters in order as they Began and were carryed on and Issued : that so I may not deceive the Reader in confounding of Things, but the Discourse may be both Plain and Easy.*

And although some may think they have Wrote in a high Stile, and done some notable Thing, yet in my Opinion they have not spoken truly in some Particulars, and in general to little Purpose : For how can History *find Credit, if in the Beginning you do not deliver plainly and clearly from whence and how you do come to the Relation which you presently intend to make of Actions ?*

As a Rule, although it hath less length and breadth, yet notwithstanding it retains the Name if it hath that

---

* The Author *Died* before the Reverend Mr. *William Hubbard* and M . *Increase Mather* Published their Accounts of the *Pequot War.*

which is proper to a Rule. When the Bones are separated from a living Creature it becomes unserviceable: So a History, if you take away Order and Truth, the rest will prove to be but a vain Narration.

I shall not make a long Discourse, nor labour to hold the Reader in doubt, using a multitude of Words, which is no sure Way to find out the Truth ; as if one should seek for Verity in the Current of Pratling, having nothing but a conceit worthy to hold the Reader in suspence : (Sed quo vado) In a word, the LORD *was as it were pleased to say* unto us, The Land of Canaan will I give unto thee tho' but few and Strangers in it : And when we went from one Nation to another, yea from one Kingdom to another, he suffered no Man to do us Wrong, but reproved Kings for our sakes : *And so through Mercy at length we were settled in Peace, to the Astonishment of all that were round about us : unto whom be ascribed all Glory and Praise for ever and ever.*

Norwich in NEW-ENGLAND,   Farewell
in *America.*

John Mason.

SOME

SOME

Grounds of the *War*

Againſt

the *Pequots*.

ABOUT the Year 1632 one Capt. *Stone* Arrived in the *Maſſachuſett* in a *Ship* from *Virginia* ; who ſhortly after was bound for *Virginia* again in a ſmall *Bark* with one Capt. *Norton* ; who ſailing into CONNECTICUT RIVER about *two Leagues* from the *Entrance* caſt Anchor ; there coming to them ſeveral *Indians* belonging to that Place whom the *Pequots* Tyranniʒed over, being a potent and warlike People, it being their Cuſtom ſo to deal with their neighbour Indians ; Capt. *Stone* having ſome occaſion with the *Dutch* who lived at a trading Houſe near *twenty Leagues* up the River, procured ſome of thoſe *Indians* to go as Pilots with *two* of his Men to the *Dutch* : But being benighted before they could come to their deſired Port, put the *Skiff* in which they went aſhore, where the *two Engliſhmen* falling aſleep, were both Murdered by their *Indian* Guides : There remaining with the *Bark* about *twelve* of the aforeſaid *Indians* ; who had in all probability formerly plotted their bloody Deſign ; and waiting an opportunity when ſome of the *Engliſh* were on
Shoar

Shoar and Capt. *Stone* afleep in his Cabbin, fet upon them and cruelly Murdered every one of them, plundered what they pleafed and funk the Bark.

Thefe *Indians* were not *native Pequots*; but had frequent recourfe unto them, to whom they tendered fome of thofe Goods, which were accepted by the *Chief Sachem* of the *Pequots*: Other of the faid Goods were tendered to NYNIGRETT *Sachem* of *Nayanticke*, who alfo received them.

The *Council* of the *Maffachufetts* being informed of their Proceedings, fent to fpeak with the *Pequots*, and had fome Treaties with them : But being unfatisfied therewith, fent forth Captain *John Endicot* Commander in Chief, with Capt. *Underhill*, Captain *Turner*, and with them *one hundred and twenty Men* ; who were firftly defigned on a Service againft a People living on *Block Ifland*, who were fubject to the *Narraganfett Sachem* ; they having taken a *Bark* of one Mr. *John Oldham*, Murdering him and all his Company : They were alfo to call the *Pequots* to an Account about the Murder of Capt. *Stone* ; who arriving at *Pequot* had fome Conference with them ; but little effected ; only one *Indian* flain and fome *Wigwams* burnt. After which, the *Pequots* grew inraged againft the *Englifh* who inhabited CONECTICOT, being but a fmall Number, about *two hundred and fifty*, who were there newly arrived ; fas alfo about *twenty Men* at SAYBROOK, under the Command of Lieutenant *Lyon Gardner*, who was there fettled by feveral Lords and Gentlemen in *England*. The *Pequots* falling violently upon them, flew diverfe Men at *Saybrook* ; keeping almoft a conftant Siege upon the Place ; fo that the *Englifh* were conftrained to keep within their pallizado *Fort*; being fo hard Befet and fometimes Affaulted, that Capt. *John Mafon* was fent by *Connecticut Colony* with *twenty Men* out of their fmall Numbers to fecure the Place : But after his coming, there did not one *Pequot* appear in view for one *Month* Space, which was the time he there remained.

In the Interim certain *Pequots* about *One Hundred* going to a Place called *Weathersfield* on *Connecticut* ; having formerly confederated with the *Indians* of that Place (as it was generally thought) lay in Ambufh for the *Englifh* ; divers of them going into a large Field adjoyning to the Town to their Labour, were there fet upon by the *Indians* : *Nine* of the *Englifh* were

killed

killed out right, with some Horses, and *two young Women* taken *Captives.*

At their Return from *Weathersfield*, they came down the *River* of *Connecticut* (Capt. *Mason* being then at *Saybrook Fort*) in *three Canoes* with about *one hundred Men*, which River of necessity they must pass: We espying them, concluded they had been acting some Mischief against us, made a Shot at them with a Piece of Ordnance, which beat off the Beak Head of one of their *Canoes*, wherein our *two Captives* were: it was at a very great distance: They then hastened, drew their *Canoes* over a narrow Beach with all speed and so got away.

Upon which the *English* were somewhat dejected: But immediately upon this, a *Court* was called and met in *Hartford* the *First* of *May* 1637, * who seriously considering their Condition, which did look very Sad, for those *Pequots* were a great People, being strongly fortified, cruel, warlike, munitioned, &c, and the *English* but an handful in comparison: But their outragious Violence against the *English*, having Murdered about *Thirty* of them, their great Pride and Insolency, constant pursuit in their malicious Courses, with their engaging other *Indians* in their Quarrel against the *English*, who had never offered them the least Wrong; who had in all likelihood Espoused all the *Indians* in the Country in their Quarrel, had not GOD by more than an ordinary Providence prevented: These Things being duly considered, with the eminent Hazard and great Peril they were in; it pelased GOD so to stir up the Hearts of all Men in general, and the *Court* in special, that they concluded some Forces should forthwith be sent out against the *Pequots*; their Grounds being Just, and necessity enforcing them to engage in an offensive and defensive *War*: the Management of which *War* we are nextly to relate.

---

* *May* 1. 1637 was *Monday.*

An

AN

Epitome or brief Hiſtory

OF THE

Pequot War.

IN the Beginning of *May* 1637 there were ſent out by CONNECTICUT CoLONY *Ninety* Men under the Command of Capt. *John Maſon* againſt the PɛQUOTS, with ONKOS an *Indian Sachem* living at *Mohegan,* † who was newly revolted from the *Pequots* ; being Shipped in one *Pink,* one *Pinnace,* and one *Shallop* ; who ſailing down the *River* of *Connecticut* fell ſeveral times a ground, the Water being very low : The *Indians* not being wonted to ſuch Things with their ſmall *Canoes,* and alſo being impatient of Delays, deſired they might be ſet on Shoar, promiſing that they would meet us at *Saybrook* ; which we granted : They haſtening to their Quarters, fell upon *Thirty or forty* of the *Enemy* near *Saybrook Fort,* and killed *ſeven* of them outright ; ‡ having only one of their's wounded, who was ſent back to *Connecticut* in a

---

† *Onkos,* uſually called *Uncas,* the *Great Sachem* of the MOHEAGS ;
‡ Mr. *Increaſe Mather* in his Hiſtory of the *Pequot War,* ſays this was on *May* 15.

Skiff: Capt. *John Underhill* also coming with him, who informed us what was performed by *Onkos* and his Men ; which we looked at as a special Providence ; for before we were some what doubtful of his Fidelity : Capt. *Underhill* then offered his Service with *nineteen* Men to go with us, if Lieutenant *Gardner* would allow of it, who was Chief Commander at *Saybrook Fort* ; which was readily approved of by Lieutenant *Gardner* and accepted by us : In lieu of them we sent back *twenty* of our Soldiers to *Connecticut.*

Upon a *Wednesday* we arrived at *Saybrook,* where we lay Windbound until *Friday* ; often consulting how and in what manner we should proceed in our Enterprize, being altogether ignorant of the Country. At length we concluded, GOD assisting us, for *Narragansett,* and so to March through their Country, which Bordered upon the *Enemy* ; where lived a great People, it being about *fifteen Leagues* beyond *Pequot* : The *Grounds* and *Reasons* of our so Acting you shall presently understand :

‘ First, *The Pequots our Enemies, kept a continual Guard*
‘ *upon the River Night and Day.*

‘ Secondly, *Their Numbers far exceeded ours ; having*
‘ sixteen Guns *with Powder and Shot, as we were inform-*
‘ *ed by the two* Capt*ies forementioned (where we declared the*
‘ *Grounds of this War) who were taken by the* Dutch *and*
‘ *restored to us at* Saybrook *; which indeed was a very*
, *friendly Office and not to be forgotton.*

‘ Thirdly, *They were on Land, and being swift on*
‘ *Foot, might much impede our Landing and possibly dis-*
‘ *hearten our Men ; we being expected only by Land, there*
‘ *being no other Place to go on Shoar but in that River,*
‘ *nearer than* Narragansett

‘ Fourthly, *By* Narragansett *we should come upon their*
‘ *Backs and possibly might surprize them unaware, at worst*
‘ *we should be on firm Land as well as they.* All which
                                                    proved

proved very fuccefsful as the Sequel may evidently demonftrate.

But yet for all this, *our Counfel* all of them except the *Captain* were at a ftand, and could not judge it meet to fail to *Narraganfett* : And indeed there was a very ftrong Ground for it ; our Commiffion limiting us to land our Men in *Pequot River* ; we had alfo the fame Order by a Letter of Inftruction fent us to *Saybrook.*

But Capt. *Mafon* apprehending an exceeding great Hazard in fo doing, for the Reafons fore mentioned, as alfo fome other which I fhall forbear to trouble you with, did therefore earneftly defire Mr. *Stone* that he would commend our Condition to the LORD, *that Night*, to direct how in what manner we fhould demean our felves in that Refpect; He being our *Chaplin* and lying aboard our *Pink,* the Captain on fhoar. In the *Morning* very early Mr. *Stone* came afhoar to the Captain's Chamber, and told him, he had done as he had defired, and was fully fatisfied to fail for *Narraganfett.* Our Council was then called, and the feveral Reafons alledged: In fine we all agreed with one accord to fail for *Narraganfett,* which the *next Morning* we put in Execution.

I declare not this to encourage any Soldiers to Act beyond their Commiffion, or contrary to it ; for in fo doing they run a double Hazard. There was a great Commander in *Belgia* who did the *States* great Service in taking a City ; but by going beyond his Commiffion loft his Life : His name was *Grubbendunk.* But if a War be Managed duly by Judgment and Difcretion as is requifit, the Shews are many times contrary to what they feem to purfue: Wherefore the more an Enterprize is diffembled and kept fecret, the more facil to put in Execution ; as the Proverb, *The fartheft way about is fometimes the neareft way home.* I fhall make bold to prefent this as my prefent Thoughts in this Cafe ; In Matters of War, thofe who are both able and faithful fhould be improved ; and then bind them not up into too narrow a Compafs :

For

For it is not possible for the wisest and ablest Senator to foresee all Accidents and Occurrents that fall out in the Management and Pursuit of a War : Nay although possibly he might be trained up in Military Affairs ; and truly much less can he have any great Knowledge who hath had but little Experience therein.   What shall I say ?   GOD led his People thro' many Difficulties and Turnings ; yet by more than an ordinary Hand of Providence he brought them to *Canaan* at last.

On *Friday Morning,* we set Sail *for* NARRAGANSETT-BAY, and on *Saturday* towards *Evening* we arrived at our desired Port, there we kept the *Sabbath.*

On the *Monday* the Wind blew so hard at North-West that we could not go on Shoar ; as also on the *Tuesday* until *Sun set* ; at which time Capt. *Mason* landed and Marched up to the Place of the *Chief Sachem's* Residence; who told the SACHEM, ' *That we had not an opportunity* ' *to acquaint him with our coming Armed in his Country* ' *sooner ; yet not doubting but it would be well accepted* ' *by him, there being Love betwixt himself and us ; well* ' *knowing also that the* Pequots *and themselves were Ene-* ' *mies, and that he could not be unacquainted with those* ' *intolerable Wrongs and Injuries these* Pequots *had lately* ' *done unto the* English ; *and that we were now come,* GOD ' *assisting, to Avenge our selves upon them ; and that we did* ' *only desire free Passage through his Country.'*   Who returned us this ANSWER, ' *That he did accept of our coming,* ' *and did also approve of our Design ; only he thought our* ' *Numbers were too weak to deal with the Enemy, who* ' *were (as he said) very great Captains and Men skilful in* ' *War.*   Thus he spake somewhat slighting of us.

On the *Wednesday Morning,* we Marched from thence to a Place called NAYANTICK, it being about *eighteen* or *twenty Miles* distant, where another of those *Narragansett Sachems* lived in a *Fort* ; it being a *Frontier* to the *Pequots.*   They carryed very proudly towards us ; not permitting any of us to come into their Fort.

We

We beholding their Carriage and the Falſhood of *Indians*, and fearing leaſt they might diſcover us to the Enemy, eſpecially they having many times ſome of their near Relations among their greateſt Foes ; we therefore cauſed a ſtrong Guard to be ſet about their *Fort*, giving Charge that no *Indian* ſhould be ſuffered to paſs in or out : We alſo informed the *Indians*, that none of them ſhould ſtir out of the *Fort* upon peril of their Lives : ſo as they would not ſuffer any of us to come into their *Fort*, ſo we would not ſuffer any of them to go out of the *Fort*.

There we quartered *that Night*, the Indians not offering to ſtir out all the while.

In the *Morning*, there came to us ſeveral of My ANTOMO† his Men, who told us, they were come to aſſiſt us in our Expedition, which encouraged divers *Indians* of that Place to Engage alſo ; who ſuddenly gathering into a Ring, one by one, making ſolemn Proteſtations how galliantly they would demean themſelves, and how many Men they would Kill.

On the *Thurſday* about *eight of the Clock* in the *Morning*, we Marched thence *towards* PEQUOT, with about *five hundred Indians*: But through the Heat of the Weather and want of Proviſions, ſome of our Men Fainted : And having Marched about *twelve Miles*, we came to *Pawcatuck-River*, at a *Ford* where our *Indians* told us the *Pequots* did uſually Fiſh ; there making an *Alta*, we ſtayed ſome ſmall time : The *Narraganſett Indians* manifeſting great Fear, in ſo much that many of them returned, although they had frequently deſpiſed us, ſaying, *That we durſt not look upon a* PEQUOT, *but themſelves would perform great Things* ; though we had often told them *that we came on purpoſe and were reſolved,* GOD *aſſiſting, to ſee the* PEQUOTS, *and to Fight with them before we*

---

† He was uſually called *Miantonimo* the Great Sachem of the *Narraganſet Indians.*

returned,

returned, though we perished. I then enquired of ONKOS, *what he thought the Indians would do?* Who said, *The* NARRAGANSETTS *would all leave us, but as for* HIM- SELF *He would never leave us*: and so it proved : For which Expreſſions and ſome other Speeches of his, I ſhall never forget him. Indeed he was a great Friend, and did great Service.

And after we had refreſhed our ſelves with our mean Commons, we Marched about *three Miles,* and came to a *Field* which had lately been planted with *IndianCorn :* There we made another *Alt,* and called our Council, ſuppoſing we drew near to the Enemy : And being in- formed by the *Indians* that the Enemy had *two Forts* almoſt impregnable; but we were not at allDiſcouraged, but rather Animated, in ſo much that we were reſolved to Aſſault both their Forts at once. But underſtanding that *one of them* was ſo remote that we could not come up with it before *Midnight,* though we Marched hard ; where- at we were much grieved, chiefly becauſe the greateſt and bloodieſt *Sachem* there reſided, whoſe Name was SASSACOUS : We were then conſtrained, being exceed- ingly ſpent in our March with extream Heat and want of Neceſſaries, to accept of the *neareſt.*

We then Marching on in a ſilent Manner, the *Indians* that remained fell all into the *Rear,* who formerly kept the *Van* ; (being poſſeſſed with great Fear) we continued our March till about *one Hour in the Night :* and coming to a *little Swamp between two Hills,* there we pitched our litttle Camp ; much wearied with hard Travail, keeping great Silence, ſuppoſing we were very near the *Fort* as our *Indians* informed us ; which proved otherwiſe : The Rocks were our Pillows ; yet Reſt was pleaſant : The *Night* proved Comfortable, being clear and MoonLight: We appointed our Guards and placed our Sentinels at ſome diſtance ; who heard the Enemy Singing at the *Fort,* who continued that Strain until Midnight, with great In- ſulting and Rejoycing, as we were afterwards informed : They ſeeing our *Pinnaces* ſail by them ſome Days before, concluded

concluded we were affraid of them and durſt not come near them ; the Burthen of their Song tending to that purpoſe.

In the *Morning*, we awaking and feeing it very light, ſuppoſing it had been day, and ſo we might have loſt our Opportunity, having purpoſed to make our Aſſault before Day ; rowſed the Men with all expedition, and briefly commended ourſelves and Deſign to Gon, thinking immediately to go to the Aſſault ; the *Indians* ſhewing us a *Path*, told us that it led directly to the *Fort.* We held on our March about *two Miles*, wondering that we came not to the *Fort*, and fearing we might be deluded : But ſeeing Corn newly planted at the Foot of a *great Hill*, ſuppoſing the *Fort* was not far off, a Champion Country being round about us ; then making a ſtand, gave the Word f r ſome of the *Indians* to come up: At length ONKOS and one WEQUOSH appeared: We demanded of them, *Where was the Fort ?* They anſwered, *On the Top of that Hill:* Then we demanded, *Where were the Reſt of the Indians ?* They anſwered, *Behind, exceedingly affraid :* We wiſhed them to tell the reſt of their Fellows, *That they ſhould by no means Fly, but ſtand at what diſtance they pleaſed, and ſee whether* ENGLISH MEN *would now Fight or not.* Then Captain *Underhill* came up, who Marched in the Rear ; and commending our ſelves to GOD divided our Men : There being *two Entrances* into the *Fort*, intending to enter both at once : Captain *Maſon* leading up to that on the *North Eaſt Side;* who approaching within one Rod, heard a Dog bark and an *Indian* crying *Owanux ! Owanux !* which is *Engliſhmen ! Engliſhmen !* We called up our Forces with all expedition, gave Fire upon them through the Pallizado ; the *Indians* being in a dead indeed their laſt Sleep : Then we wheeling off fell upon the *main Entrance*, which was blocked up with Buſhes about Breaſt high, over which the *Captain* paſſed, intending to make good the Entrance, encouraging the reſt to follow. Lieutenant *Seeley* endeavoured to enter ; but being ſomewhat cumbred, ſtepped back and pulled out the Buſhes and ſo entred,

D

tred, and with him about *sixteen Men*: We had formerly concluded to destroy them by the Sword and save the Plunder.

Whereupon Captain *Mason* seeing no *Indians*, entred a *Wigwam*; where he was beset with many *Indians*, waiting all opportunities to lay Hands on him, but could not prevail. At length *William Heydon* espying the Breach in the *Wigwam*, supposing some *English* might be there, entred, but in his Entrance fell over a dead *Indian*; but speedily recovering himself, the *Indians* some fled, others crept under their Beds: The *Captain* going out of the *Wigwam* saw many *Indians* in the Lane or Street; he making towards them, they fled, were pursued to the End of the Lane, where they were met by *Edward Pattison, Thomas Barber*, with some others; where *seven* of them were Slain, as they said. The *Captain* facing about, Marched a slow Pace up the Lane he came down, perceiving himself very much out of Breath; and coming to the other End near the Place where he first entred, saw *two Soldiers* standing close to the Pallizado with their Swords pointed to the Ground: The *Captain* told them that *We should never kill them after that manner*: The *Captain* also said, WE MUST BURN THEM; and immediately stepping into the *Wigwam* where he had been before, brought out a Fire Brand, and putting it into the Matts with which they were covered, set the *Wigwams* on Fire. Lieutenant *Thomas Bull* and *Nicholas Omsted* beholding, came up; and when it was throughly kindled, the *Indians* ran as Men most dreadfully Amazed.

And indeed such a dreadful Terror did the ALMIGHTY let fall upon their Spirits, that they would fly from us and run into the very Flames, where many of them perished. And when the *Fort* was throughly Fired, Command was given, that all should fall off and surround the *Fort*; which was readily attended by all; only one *Arthur Smith* being so wounded that he could not move out of the

the Place, who was happily efpied by Lieutenant *Bull*, and by him refcued.

The Fire was kindled on the *North Eaſt Side* to wind-ward ; which did fwiftly over run the *Fort*, to the ex-tream Amazement of the Enemy, and great Rejoycing of our felves. Some of them climbing to the Top of the Palizado ; others of them running into the very Flames ; many of them gathering to windward, lay pelting at us with their Arrows ; and we repayed them with our fmall Shot : Others of the Stouteſt iſſued forth, as we did guefs, to the Number of *Forty*, who periſhed by the Sword.

What I have formerly faid, is according to my own Knowlege, there being fufficient living Teſtimony to every Particular.

But in reference to Captain *Underhill* and his Parties acting in this Aſſault, I can only intimate as we were informed by fome of themfelves immediately after the Fight, Thus *They* Marching up to the *Entrance* on the *South Weſt Side*, there made fome Paufe ; a valiant, refo-lute Gentleman, one Mr HEDGE, ſtepping towards the Gate, faying, *If we may not Enter, wherefore came we hear* ; and immediately endeavoured toEnter ; but was oppofed by a ſturdy *Indian* which did impede his Entrance : but the *Indian* being ſlain by himfelf and Serjeant *Davis*, Mr. *Hedge* Entred the *Fort* with fome others ; but the *Fort* being on Fire, the Smoak and Flames were fo violent that they were conſtrained to defert the *Fort*.

Thus were they now at their Wits End, who not many Hours before exalted themfelves in their great Pride, threatning and refolving the utter Ruin and Deſtruction of all the *Engliſh*, Exulting and Rejoycing with Songs and Dances : But GOD was above them, who laughed his Enemies and the Enemies of his People to Scorn, making them as a fiery Oven : Thus were the Stout Hearted fpoiled, having ſlept their laſt Sleep, and none of their

Men

Men could find their Hands : Thus did the LORD judge among the Heathen, filling the Place with dead Bodies!

And here we may see the just Judgment of GOD, in sending even the very *Night before* this Assault, *One hundred and fifty Men* from their other *Fort*, to join with them of that Place, who were designed as some of themselves reported to go forth against the *English*, at that very Instant when this heavy Stroak came upon them, where they perished with their Fellows. So that the Mischief they intended to us, came upon their own Pate: They were taken in their own Snare, and we through Mercy escaped. And thus in *little more than one Hour's space* was their impregnable *Fort* with themselves utterly Destroyed, to the Number of *six* or *seven Hundred*, as some of themselves confessed. There were only *seven* taken *Captive* & about *seven escaped.* *

Of the *English*, there were *two Slain* outright, and about *twenty Wounded*: Some Fainted by reason of the sharpness of the Weather, it being a cool Morning & the want of such Comforts & Necessaries as were needful in such a Case ; especially our *Chyrurgeon* was much wanting, whom we left with our *Barks* in *Narragansett Bay*, who had Order there to remain until the *Night* before our intended Assault.

And thereupon grew many *Difficulties* : Our Provision and Munition near spent ; we in the Enemies Country, who did far exceed us in Number, being much inraged; all our *Indians*, except ONKOS, deserting us ; our *Pinnaces* at a great distance from us, and when they would come we were uncertain.

But as we were consulting what Course to take, it pleased GOD to discover our *Vessels* to us before a fair

---

* The Place of the Fort being called MISTICK, this Fight was called MISTICK-FIGHT : And Mr. *Increase Mather*, from a *Manuscript* He met with, tells us ; It was on *Friday*, May 26. 1637, a *memorable Day* !

Gale

Gale of Wind failing into *Pequot Harbour*, to our great Rejoycing.

We had no fooner difcovered our *Veffels*, bnt immediately came up the *Enemy* from the OTHER FORT; *Three Hundred or more* as we conceived. The *Captain* lead out *a File or two* of Men to Skirmifh with them, chiefly to try what Temper they were of, who put them to a ftand: we being much encouraged thereat, prefently prepared to March towards our Veffels: *Four* or *Five* of our Men were fo wounded that they muft be carried with the Arms of *twenty* more. We alfo being faint, were conftrained to put *four* to *one* Man, with the Arms of the reft that were wounded to others; fo that we had not above *forty* Men free: at length we hired feveral *Indians*, who eafed us of that Burthen in carrying of our wounded Men. And Marching about *one quarter of a Mile*; the Enemy coming up to the Place where the *Fort* was, and beholding what was done, ftamped and tore the Hair from their Heads: And after a little fpace, came mounting down the *Hill* upon us, in a full career, as if they would over run us: But when they came within Shot, the Rear faced about, giving Fire upon them: Some of them being Shot, made the reft more wary: Yet they held on running to and fro, and fhooting their Arrows at Random. There was at the *Foot of the Hill* a *fmall Brock*, where we refted and refrefhed our felves, having by that time taught them a little more Manners than to difturb us.

We then Marched on towards *Pequot.Harbour*; and falling upon feveral *Wigwams*, burnt them: The Enemy ftill following us in the Rear, which was to windward, though to little purpofe; yet fome of them lay in Ambufh behind Rocks and Trees, often fhooting at us, yet through Mercy touched not one of us: And as we came to any Swamp or Thicket, we made fome Shot to clear the Paffage. Some of them fell with our Shot; and probably more might, but for want of Munition: But when any of them fell, our *Indians* would give a
great

great Shout, and then would they take so much Courage
as to fetch their Heads. And thus we continued, until
we came within *two Miles* of *Pequot Harbour*; where
the Enemy gathered together and left us : we Marching
on to the *Top* of an *Hill* adjoining to the Harbour, with
our Colours flying ; having left our Drum at the Place
of our Rendezvous the *Night before :* We seeing our
Vessels there Riding at Anchor, to our great Rejoycing,
and came to the *Water-Side*, we there sat down in Quiet.

Captain *Patrick* being Arrived there with our *Vessels*,
who as we were informed was sent with *Forty Men* by
the *Massachusetts* Colony, upon some Service against the
Block Islanders : Who coming to the Shore in our Shallop with all his Company, as he said, to Rescue us, supposing we were pursued, though there did not appear
any the least sign of such a Thing.

But we could not prevail with Him by any Means to
put his Men ashore, that so we might carry our Wounded
Men a Board ; although it was our own Boat in which
he was : We were very much Troubled ; but knew not
how to help our selves. At length we were fetched
a Board to the great Rejoycing of our Friends.

Shortly after our coming a Board, there fell out a great
Contest between Captain *Underhill* and Capt. *Patrick* :
Captain *Underhill* claiming an Interest in the Bark where
Captain *Patrick* was, which indeed was *Underhill's*
Right ; the Contest grew to a great Heighth. At length
we propounded, that if *Patrick* would Ride there with
that *Bark* in Contention, and secure the *Narraganset
Indians*, it being also the Place of Rendezvous to those
Vessels that were expected from *Massachuset*, until we
Transported our Wounded Men to *Saybrock* five *Leagues*
distant ; then we wou'd immediately return our *Pink* to
convey the *Narragansetts* home : The which Captain
Patrick seemed very readily to accept.

Captain

Captain *Underhill* soon after set sail in one of our *Barks* for *Saybrook :* But before he was out of Sight ; Captain *Patrick* signified by Writing, that he could not attend that Service, but he must wait for the *Bay Vessels* at *Saybrook,* wishing us, having the Honour of that Service to compleat it, by securing the *Narragansett Indians* ; which at first seemed very Difficult, if not Impossible : For our *Pink* could not receive them, and to march by *Land* was very Dangerous ; it being near *twenty Miles* in the Enemies Country, our Numbers being much weakened, we were then about *twenty Men*, the rest we had sent home for fear of the *Pequots* Invasion. But absolutely necessitated to March by Land, we hasted ashore, with our *Indians* and small Numbers. Captain *Patrick* seeing what we intended, came ashore also with his Men ; although in truth we did not desire or delight in his Company, and so we plainly told him : However he would and did March a long with us.

About the *midway* between that and *Saybrook,* we fell upon a People called *Nayanticks,* belonging to the *Pequots,* who fled to a Swamp for Refuge : They hearing or espying of us, fled : We pursued them a while by the Track as long as they kept together : But being much spent with former Travel, and the *Sabbath* drawing on, it being about *Two* or *Three* of the *Clock* on the *Saturday* in the *Afternoon* ; we leaving our Pursuit, hasted towards *Saybrook,* about *Sun set* we Arrived at *Connecticut River Side* ; being nobly Entertained by Lieutenant *Gardner* with many great Guns : But were forced there to Quarter that Night : On the Morrow we were all fetched over to *Saybrook,* receiving many Courtesies from Lieut. *Gardner.*

And when we had taken Order for the safe Conduct of the *Narragansett Indians,* we repaired to the Place of our Abode : where we were Entertained with great Triumph and Rejoycing and Praising God for his Goodness to us, in succeeding our weak Endeavours, in Crowning us with Success, and restoring of us with so little Loss.
Thus

Thus was God seen in the Mount, Crushing his proud Ene-
mies and the Enemies of his People : They who were ere
while a Terror to all that were round about them, who
resolved to Destroy all the ENGLISH *and to Root their*
very Name out of this Country, should by such weak Means,
even SEVENTY SEVEN *(there being no more at the* FORT *)*
bring the Mischief they plotted, and the Violence they
offered and exercised, upon their own Heads in a Moment ;
burning them up in the Fire of his Wrath, and dunging the
Ground with their Flesh: It was the LORD's *Doings, and*
it is marvellous in our Eyes ! It is HE *that hath made his*
Work wonderful, and therefore ought to be remembred.

Immediately the whole Body of *Pequots* repaired to
that Fort where SASSACOUS the *Chief Sachem* did reside ;
charging him that he was the only Cause of all the
Troubles that had befallen them ; and therefore they
would Destroy both him and his : But by the Intreaty of
their *Counsellors* they spared his Life ; and consulting what
Course to take, concluded *there was no abiding any longer*
in their Country, and so resolved *to fly into several Parts.*
The greatest Body of them went towards MANHATANCE:*
And passing over *Connecticut*, they met with *three*
English Men in a *Shallop* going for *Saybrook*, whom they
slew : The *English* Fought very stoutly, as themselves
confessed, Wounding many of the Enemy.

About a *Fortnight* after our *Return* home, which was
about one *Month* after the *Fight* at MISTICK, there
Arrived in PEQUOT RIVER several *Vessels* from the MAS-
SACHUSETS, Captain *Israel Stoughton* being Commander
in Chief ; and with him about *One hundred and twenty Men* ;
being sent by that Colony to pursue the War against the
Pequots: The Enemy being all fled before they came,
except some few Stragglers, who were surprised by the *Mo-*
heags and others of the *Indians*, and by them delivered to
the *Massachusets Soldiers.*

---

* I suppose this the same which is sometimes called *Manhatan* or
Manhatees ; which is since called New-York.

Connecticut

Connecticut Colony being informed hereof, fent forthwith *forty Men*, Captain *Mason* being Chief Commander; with fome other Gent, to meet thofe of the *Maffachufetts*, to confider what was neceffary to be attended refpecting the future : Who meeting with them of the *Maffachufetts* in *Pequot Harbour* ; after fome time of confultation, concluded to purfue thofe *Pequots* that were fled towards *Manhatance*, and fo forthwith Marched after them, difcovering feveral Places where they Rendezvoufed and lodged not far diftant from their feveral R:moves ; making but little hafte, by reafon of their Children, and want of Provifion ; being forced to dig for Clams, and to procure fuch other things as the Wildernefs afforded : Our *Veffels* failing along by the Shore. In about the fpace of *three Days* we all Arrived at *New Haven Harbour*, then called *Quinnypiag*. And feeing a great Smoak in the Woods not far diftant, we fuppofing fome of the *Pequots* our Enemies might be there ; we haftened afhore, but quickly difcovered them to be *Connecticut Indians*. Then we returned aboard our Veffels, where we ftayed fome fhort time, having fent a *Pequot Captive* upon difcovery, we named him *Luz* ; who brought us Tydings of the Enemy, which proved true; fo faithful was he to us, though againft his own Nation. Such was the Terror of the *Englifh* upon them ; that a *Moheage Indian* named *Jack Eatow* going afhore at that time, met with *three Pequots*, took *two* of them and brought them aboard.

We then haftened our March towards the Place where the Enemy was : And coming into a Corn Field, feveral of the *Englifh* efpyed fome *Indians*, who fled from them : They purfued them ; and coming to the Top of an Hill, faw feveral *Wigwams* juft oppofite, only a *Swamp* intervening, which was almoft divided in two Parts. Serjeant *Palmer* haftening with about *twelve Men* who were under his Command to furround the fmaller Part of the *Swamp*, that fo He might prevent the *Indians* flying ; Enfign *Danport*,* Serjeant *Jeffries* &c, entering the Swamp,

---

* It fhould be *Davenport*, who was afterwards *Captain* of th^e *Caftle* in *Bofton* Harbour.

D   intended

intended to have gone to the *Wigwams,* were there set
upon by several *Indians,* who in all probability were
deterred by Serjeant *Palmer.* In this Skirmish the *English*
slew but few ; *two* or *three* of themselves were Wounded :
The rest of the *English* coming up, the *Swamp* was
surrounded.

Our *Council* being called, and the *Question* propounded,
How we should proceed, Captain *Patrick* advised that we
should cut down the *Swamp* ; there being many *Indian
Hatchets* taken, Captain *Traske* concurring with him; but
was opposed by others: Then we must pallizado the
Swamp ; which was also opposed: Then they would have
a Hedge made like those of *Gotham* ; all which was
judged by some almost impossible, and to no purpose,
and that for several Reasons, and therefore strongly opposed But some others advised to force the *Swamp,*
having time enough, it being about *three* of the *Clock*
in the *Afternoon* : But that being opposed, it was then
propounded to draw up our Men close to the *Swamp,*
which would much have lessened the Circumference ; and
with all to fill up the open Passages with Bushes, that so
we might secure them until the *Morning,* and then we
might consider further about it. But neither of these
would pass ; so different were our Apprehensions ; which
was very grievous to some of us, who concluded the *Indians* would make an Escape in the *Night,* as easily they
might and did : We keeping at a great distance, what
better could be expected? Yet Captain *Mason* took
Order that the Narrow in the *Swamp* should be cut thro' ;
which did much shorten our Leaguer· It was resolutely
performed by Serjeant *Davis.*

We being loth to destroy *Women* and *Children,* as also
the *Indians* belonging to that Place ; whereupon Mr.
Tho. Stanton a Man well acquainted with *Indian Language*
and Manners, offered his Service to go into the *Swamp*
and treat with them : To which we were somewhat backward, by reason of some Hazard and Danger he might
be exposed unto : But his importunity prevailed : Who
going to them, did in a short time return to us, with
near *Two Hundred old Men, Women* and *Children* ; who
delivered

delivered themfelves to the Mercy of the *Englifh.* And fo *Night* drawing on, we beleaguered them as ftrongly as we could. About *half an Hour before Day,* the *Indians* that were in the *Swamp* attempted to break through Captain *Patrick's Quarters* ; but were beaten back feveral times ; they making a *great Noife,* as their Manner is at fuch Times, it founded round about our Leaguer : Whereupon Captain *Mafon* fent Serjeant *Stares* to inquire into the Caufe, and alfo to affift if need required ; Capt. *Traske* coming alfo in to their Affiftance : But the Tumult growing to a very great Heighth, we raifed our Siege; and Marching up to the Place, at a Turning of the *Swamp* the *Indians* were forcing out upon us ; but we fent them back by our fmall Shot.

We waiting a little for a fecond Attempt ; the *Indians* in the mean time facing about, preffed violently upon Captain *Patrick,* breaking through his Quarters, and fo efcaped. They were about *fixty* or *feventy* as we were informed. We afterwards fearched the *Swamp,* & found but few *Slain.* The *Captives* we took were about *One Hundred and Eighty* ; whom we divided, intending to keep them as *Servants,* but they could not endure that Yoke ; few of them continuing any confiderable time with their Mafters.

Thus did the LORD *fcatter his Enemies with his ftrong Arm !* The *Pequots* now became a Prey to all *Indians.* Happy were they that could bring in their Heads to the *Englifh :* Of which there came almoft daily to *Winfor,* or *Hartford* But the *Pequots* growing weary hereof, fent fome of the Chief that furvived to *mediate* with the *Englifh* ; offering that *If they might but enjoy their Lives, they would become the* Englifh *Vaffals, to difpofe of them as they pleafed.* Which was granted them. Whereupon ONKOS and MYANTONIMO were fent for ; who with the *Pequots* met at *Hartford.* The *Pequots* being demanded, *How many of them were then living ?* Anfwered, about *One Hundred and Eighty,* or *Two Hundred.* There were then given to ONKOS, Sachem of MONHEAG, *Eighty* ; to

MYAN-

MYANTONIMO, Sachem of NARRAGANSETT, *Eighty*; and to NYNIGRETT, † *Twenty*, when he should satisfy for a *Mare* of *Edward Pomroye's* killed by his Men. The *Pequots* were then bound by COVENANT, *That none should inhabit their native Country, nor should any of them be called* PEQUOTS *any more, but* MOHEAGS *and* NARRAGANSETTS *for ever.* Shortly after, about *Forty* of them went to *Moheag*; others went to *Long Island*; the rest settled at *Pawcatuck*, a Place in *Pequot Country*, contrary to their late Covenant and Agreement with the *English*.

Which *Connecticut* taking into Consideration, and well weighing the several Inconveniences that might ensue; for the Prevention whereof, they sent out *forty Men* under the Command of Captain *John Mason*, to supplant them, by burning their *Wigwams*, and bringing away their *Corn*, except they would desert the Place : ONKOS with about *One Hundred* of *his Men* in *twenty Canoes*, going also to assist in the Service. As we sailed into *Pawcatuck-Bay* We met with *three* of those *Indians*, whom we sent to inform the rest with the end of our coming, and also that we desired to speak with some of them : They promised speedily to return us an Answer, but never came to us more.

We run our *Vessel* up into a *small River*, and by reason of Flatts were forced to land on the *West Side*; their *Wigwams* being on the *East* just opposite, where we could see the *Indians* running up and down Jeering of us. But we meeting with a *narrow Place* in the *River* between *two Rocks*, drew up our *Indians Canoes*, and got suddenly over sooner than we were expected or desired; Marching immediately up to their *Wigwams*; the *Indians* being all fled, except some old People that could not.

We were so suddenly upon them that they had not time to convey away their Goods : We viewed their Corn,

---

† He was usually called NINNICRAFT.

whereof

whereof there was Plenty, it being their time of *Harvest*: And coming down to the Water Side to our Pinnace with *half* of ONKOS's his *Men*, the rest being plundering the *Wigwams* ; we looking towards a *Hill* not far remote, we espyed about *sixty Indians* running towards us; we supposing they were our absent Men, the *Moheags* that were with us not speaking one word, nor moving towards them until the other came within *thirty* or *forty Paces* of them ; then they run and met them and fell on pell mell striking and cutting with Bows, Hatchets, Knives, &c, after their feeble Manner : Indeed it did hardly deserve the Name of *Fighting*. We then endeavoured to get between them and the Woods, that so we might prevent their flying ; which they perceiving, endeavoured speedily to get off under the *Beach* : We made no Shot at them, nor any hostile Attempt upon them. Only *seven* of them who were NYNIGRETT's *Men*, were taken. Some of them growing very outragious, whom we intended to have made shorter by the Head ; and being about to put it in Execution; one *Otash* a Sachem of *Narragansett*, Brother to MYANTONIMO stepping forth, told the *Captain, They were his Brother's Men, and that he was a Friend to the* English, *and if we would spare their Lives we should have as many Murtherers Heads in lieu of them which should be delivered to the* English. We considering that there was no Blood shed as yet, and that it tended to Peace and Mercy, granted his Desire ; and so delivered them to ONKOS to secure them until his Engagement was performed, because our *Prison* had been very much pestered with such Creatures.

We then drew our *Bark* into a *Creek*, the better to defend her ; for there were *many Hundreds* within *five Miles* waiting upon us. There we Quartered *that Night* : In the *Morning* as soon as it was Light, there appeared in Arms at least *Three Hundred Indians* on the other Side the *Creek* : Upon which we stood to our Arms ; which they perceiving, some of them fled, others crept behind the Rocks and Trees, not one of them to be seen. We then called to them, saying, *We desired to speak with them,*
and

and that we would down our Arms for that end : Whereupon they ſtood up: We then informed them, *That the* Pequots *had violated their Promiſe with the* Engliſh, *in that they were not there to inhabit, and that we were ſent to ſupplant them :* They anſwered ſaying, *The* Pequots *were good Men, their Friends, and they would Fight for them, and protect them :* At which we were ſomewhat moved, and told them, *It was not far to the Head of the* Creek *where we would meet them, and then they might try what they could do in that Reſpect.*

They then replyed, *That they would not Fight with* ENGLISH MEN, *for they were* SPIRITS, *but would Fight with* ONKOS. We replyed, *That we thought it was too early for them to Fight, but they might take their opportunity ; we ſhould be burning* Wigwams, *and carrying Corn aboard all that Day.* And preſently beating up our Drum, we Fired the *Wigwams* in their View : And as we Marched, there were *two Indians* ſtanding upon a *Hill* jeering and reviling of us : Mr. *Thomas Stanton* our Interpreter, Marching at Liberty, deſired to make a Shot at them ; the *Captain* demanding of the *Indians, What they were ?* Who ſaid, *They were Murtherers :* Then the ſaid *Stanton* having leave, let fly, Shot one of them through both his Thighs ; which was to our Wonderment, it being at ſuch a vaſt diſtance.

We then loaded our *Bark* with Corn ; and our *Indians* their *Canoes :* And *thirty* more which we had taken, with Kittles, Trays, Matts, and other *Indian* Luggage. That *Night* we went all aboard, & ſet Sail homeward : It pleaſed GOD in a ſhort Time to bring us all in ſafety to the Place of our Abode ; although we ſtrook and ſtuck upon a Rock. The Way and Manner how GOD dealt with us in our Delivery was very Remarkable : The Story would be ſomewhat long to trouble you with at this time ; and therefore I ſhall forbear.

Thus we may ſee, *How the Face of* GOD *is ſet againſt them that do Evil, to cut off the Remembrance of them from*
the

the Earth. Our Tongue shall talk of thy Righteousness all the Day long ; for they are confounded, they are bro't to Shame that sought our Hurt ! Blessed be the LORD GOD *of Israel, who only doth wondrous Things ; and blessed be his holy Name for ever : Let the whole Earth be filled with his Glory ! Thus the* LORD *was pleased to smite our Enemies in the hinder Parts, and to give us their Land for an Inheritance : Who remembred us in our low Estate, and redeemed us out of our Enemies Hands : Let us therefore praise the* LORD *for his Goodness and his wonderful Works to the Children of Men !*

ADDITION·

I shall add a Word or two by way of COMENT.

OUR *Commons* were very short, there being a general scarcity throughout the *Colony* of all sorts of Provision, it being upon our first Arrival at the Place. We had but one Pint of strong Liquors among us in our whole March, but what the Wilderness afforded ; (the Bottle of Liquor being in my Hand) & when it was empty, the very smelling to the Bottle would presently recover such as Fainted away, which happened by the extremity of the Heat : And thus we Marched on in an uncoath and unknown Path to the *English*, though much frequented by *Indians.* And was not the Finger of GOD in all this ? By his special Providence to lead us along in the Way we should go : Nay though we knew not where their Forts were, how far it was to them, nor the Way that led to them, but by what we had from our *Indian* Guides ; whom we could not confide in, but looked at them as uncertain : And yet notwithstanding all our Doubts, we should be brought on the very fittest Season ; nay and which is yet more, that we should be carried in our March among a treacherous and perfidious People, yea in our alledgment so near the Enemy, all Night in so populous a Country, and not the least Notice of us ; seemeth somewhat strange, and more than ordinary : Nay that we should come to their very Doors : *What shall I say ?* GOD was pleased to hide us in the Hollow of his Hand : I still rememb

remember a Speech of Mr. HOOKER at our going aboard ;
THAT THEY SHOULD BE BREAD FOR US. And thus when
the LORD turned the Captivity of his People, and turned the
Wheel upon their Enemies ; we were like Men in a Dream ; then
was our Mouth filled with Laughter, and our Tongues with Singing ; thus we may say the LORD hath done great Things for us
among the Heathen, whereof we are glad. Praise ye the LORD !

I shall mention two or three *special Providences* that GOD was
pleased to vouchsafe to *Particular Men*; viz. *two Men*, being one Man's
Servants, namely, *John Dier* and *Thomas Stiles*, were both of them
Shot in the Knots of their Handkerchiefs, being about their Necks,
and received no Hurt. Lieutenant *Seeley* was Shot in the Eyebrew
with a flat headed Arrow, the Point turning downwards : I pulled
it out my self. Lieutenant *Bull* had an Arrow Shot into a hard
piece of Cheese, having no other Defence : Which may verify the
old Saying, *A little Armour would serve if a Man knew where to place
it*. Many such Providences happened ; some respecting my self ;
but since there is none that Witness to them, I shall forbear to
mention them.

The *Year ensuing*, the *Colony* being in extream Want of Provision, many giving *twelve Shillings* for *one Bushel* of *Indian Corn*; the *Court*
of *Connecticut* imploying Captain *Mason*, Mr *William Wadsworth*
and Deacon *Stebbin*, to try what Providence would afford, for their
Relief in this great Straight : Who notwithstanding some dis-
couragement they met with from some *English*, went to a Place
called *Pocomtuck* : ‡ where they procured so much *Corn* at reason-
able Rates, that the *Indians* brought down to *Hartford* and *Windsor*,
FIFTY CANOES laden with *Corn* at one time. Never was the like
known to this Day ! So although the LORD was pleased to shew
his People hard Things ; yet did he execute Judgment for the
Oppressed, and gave Food to the Hungry. O let us meditate on
the Great Works of GOD : Ascribing all Blessing and Praise to
his Great Name, for all his Great Goodness and Salvation ! *Amen,
Amen.*

---

‡ Since called *Deerfield*.

FINIS.